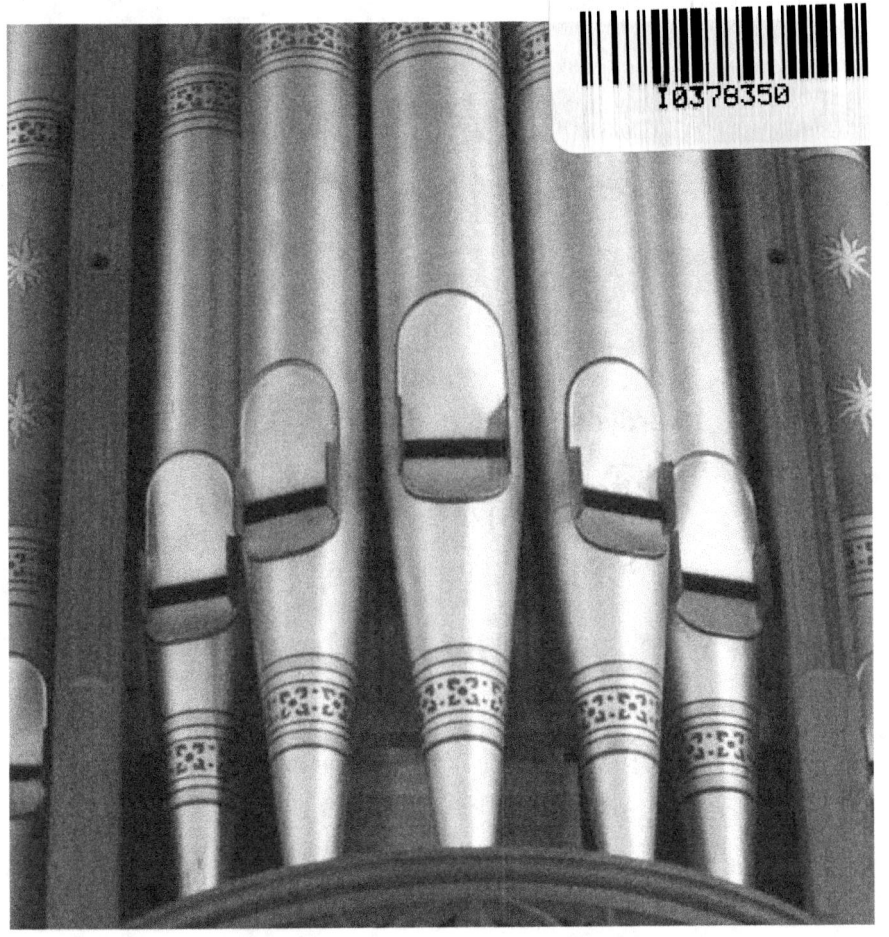

Music Notes from Croydon Minster
by David Morgan

Published by
Filament Publishing Ltd
16 Croydon Road, Beddington, Croydon,
Surrey, CR0 4PA, United Kingdom.
+44(0)20 8688 2598
www.filamentpublishing.com

© David Morgan 2017

Photographs by David Morgan, Steve O'Sullivan,
Nela Pecher and Chris Day

ISBN 978-1-911425-85-4

Printed by IngramSpark

The right of David Morgan to be identified as the author of this work has been asserted by him in accordance with the Designs and Copyright Act 1988.

All rights reserved. This book may not be copied in any way without the prior written permission of the publishers.

About the Author

David Morgan

The author was born in Lowestoft, Suffolk but spent his years of study and teaching in South London. Recently retired after a successful 12-year headship in Croydon, David is now able to spend more time writing, researching local history and singing in the Croydon Minster choir. He leads tours of the church and the Whitgift Almshouses.

In 2016, he also published a companion book to this, **Minster Tales.**

Table of Contents

Foreword by Ronny Krippner	7
Prelude by David Morgan	9
A sustained Note about Andrew Cantrill	13
A staccato Note about Charles Smith	23
A sustained Note about F. Rowland Tims	27
A staccato Note about James Harborough	33
A sustained Note about Frederick Cambridge	37
A staccato Note about John Rhodes	43
A sustained Note about H. Leslie Smith	47
A staccato Note about James Bartleman	53
A sustained Note about John Avery	57
Specification of the 1794 Avery Organ	63
A staccato Note about Leslie Tasker	65
A sustained Note about John Pyke Hullah	73
A staccato Note about Frederick Kill Harford	78
A staccato Note about Derek Holman	83
A sustained Note about Thomas Miller	84
A staccato Note about Ray Massey	88
A sustained Note about Thomas Walmisley	89
A staccato Note about Michael Fleming	92
A sustained Note about Martin How	93

INTERIOR VIEW OF CROYDON CHURCH.
(DRAWN BEFORE THE RESTORATION.)

Foreword by Ronny Krippner

Croydon Minster has had a rich musical tradition for centuries and this is most evident in the quality of musicians that held the post of Organist here. We are particularly proud of our association with Thomas Attwood Walmisley (1815-1856) who was Organist at Croydon Minster for three years before moving on to become Organist at Trinity College Cambridge. His Evening Service in D Minor is known (and sung) throughout the English-speaking world and has helped spread Walmisley's fame.

The German composer Felix Mendelssohn, a contemporary of Walmisley, visited the Minster and played the organ there. The thought of Mendelssohn improvising on the old Minster Organ is rather intriguing! Following Walmisley's appointment, there have been many illustrious Organists at the Minster who have left a legacy and the Minster's thriving choral programme is testament to that. Today, our Boys' Choir, Girls' Choir, Lay Clerks and Choral Scholars involve over 90 singers from all walks of life and sing in five choral services per week during term-time. Our strong connection with Whitgift School and Old Palace School has proven particularly successful! The future is looking bright for music at Croydon Minster, so it is only appropriate to look at its past – enjoy this wonderful book.

Ronny Krippner
Organist & Director of Music
Croydon Minster

Prelude
by David Morgan

Like any composition, the musical life of Croydon Minster (which until 2011 was known as Croydon Parish Church) contains many notes. Some have been brief, hanging in the air for only a moment. Others have resounded down the years. A few have lasted for almost a lifetime.

Some of this book's characters appear fleetingly and their stories are part of the larger tale of the Minster's music either briefly, through a single event or in one most interesting story, in childhood. These are like little bursts of sound, so I have described them as 'staccato Notes', using the musical term for a note played for a brief moment only. Other musicians have made the Minster their lasting home, so that their musical and personal history has intertwined with that of the building and with Croydon itself. Theirs are the 'sustained Notes' that still resound around us.

But I don't believe that the longer Notes are more important than those which are brief. All have fascinated me as I have learned and written about them, and just as in music, each is part of a larger harmony. Without any one of them, that harmony would be diminished. Every Note has its part to play.

As a current Lay Clerk in the Minster choir I have a particular responsibility for those deep resonant bass notes that define

and support the harmony. I am privileged to have been part of a choir with a range of talented individuals. I have listened and watched broadcasts from Kings College Cambridge with interest over the last few years to follow the progress of a former Minster chorister who sang there.

Processing into the choir stalls for the services, we are reminded of the choral traditions which have been built up over many years. The wooden board upon which the names of former organists and directors of music have been painted in gold serves as a reminder that many prominent musicians spent their early years here. Indeed, one person visiting the church before a recent concert commented that the list read 'like a Who's Who of twentieth century church music.'

Once stationed in the choir stalls themselves, there can be seen small brass plaques screwed to the pews on which are inscribed the names of long serving choir members from years gone by. Organists and singers have combined over the years to produce a glorious and inspirational sound which has elevated and inspired worship in this church, a polyphony not only for the moment but through the years.

It is my particular interest in, and love of, that music which has motivated me to write this book.

A sustained Note about Andrew Cantrill.

Andrew was organist and Master of the Choristers at Croydon Minster from 2008-2012. During his time at the Minster, however, not everyone knew of his globetrotting past or the stellar figures from the world's musical and entertainment community who featured in it. His is a Note of considerable glamour, which adds prestige and excitement to the Minster's musical life.

Could there be a connection between Croydon Minster and the international hit film The Lord of the Rings, directed by Peter Jackson and of course based on the books by J.R.R. Tolkien? Surprisingly, the answer is yes... and the answer is musical!

Most people have a favourite piece of music or two from films that they have seen and enjoyed. Whether it is the spiky sounds from Hitchcock's Psycho or the opening notes from the spaghetti Western, The Good, the Bad and the Ugly, film scores are an important part of our musical landscape. Composers such as John Williams, Hans Zimmer and Ennio Morricone have made their names penning chords and melodies for film sequences.

An increasing number of cinema screenings in concert halls now have a sound track played live by an orchestra and choir in order to create a special atmosphere. Imagine, then, a live concert of music of the sound track from The Lord of the Rings films with the composer Howard Shore conducting. The venue is the Michael Fowler Centre, Wellington, New Zealand. In the audience for this stellar event is Drew (Andrew) Cantrill, at that time musical director of the choirs involved but better known (to us, at least) as a future choir master of Croydon Minster.

Howard Shore

Drew finds himself sitting next to Viggo Mortensen who plays the heroic character Aragorn in the film. Some of the young choristers would have liked Drew to have passed on some of the stardust after shaking his hand before turning to shake theirs!

In attendance on this night, together with a number of New Zealand's dignitaries, there are also other stars from the film trilogy. What an occasion!

This concert was one of many highlights that Drew looks back on during his time working in New Zealand. It was not something that he envisaged as he touched down on the tarmac of Wellington International Airport to be met by a car ready to whisk him off to his new home in the Cathedral Close. Whatever nerves he felt as he approached his new post must have been heightened by the fact that he had never even been to New Zealand before his arrival. Even his job interview with the cathedral's dean took place in Birmingham. But there he was, ready to start work the next day, despite his jetlag.

For a new organist and music director it is vital to understand the acoustic of the building in which you are to make music. Drew walked into the large cathedral made from reinforced concrete, the material best suited to withstanding earthquakes, and was immediately impressed by the immense space which the design created. Although it was a plain building, the acoustic was excellent. 'Even when the choir was not quite at its best,' smiled Drew, 'the acoustic made the sound that bit better.'

He found he had inherited an adult choir, largely made up of students, who sang on Thursdays and Sundays. He quickly set about establishing a cathedral choir for younger singers too. There was no way that the cathedral wished to develop single sex choirs, so he recruited both boys and girls into this new group which soon began to sing evensong on a Tuesday.

Other resources at his disposal for larger events included the Orpheus Choir of Wellington, of which he was the conductor for the five years he lived there, and the New Zealand Symphony Orchestra.

Returning to the Lord of the Rings theme for a moment, one can quickly imagine the rolling green landscapes together with snow-topped mountain ranges associated with the film. Drew was to make numerous journeys over such terrain during his years in New Zealand. There are eight Anglican cathedrals in the country with St. Paul's occupying a special place within the parliamentary precinct. He visited all these cathedrals for recitals and workshops, crisscrossing the two islands on many occasions as he did so.

Drew also spent time teaching at the Massey University Conservatorium of Music. Wellington, situated at the southern end of the North Island and serving as Drew's base, is certainly not large, having a population close to 400,000 people, but it is the centre of government with a thriving community of politicians and diplomats. Being in such a centre was to lead to another of Drew's highlights during his tenure there.

When the Queen visits New Zealand, it is to Wellington that she usually heads. On her visit of 2002 she attended a service at St Paul's to celebrate and dedicate the final parts of the cathedral that had recently been completed. To plan and then to play and conduct for a service which the Queen attends is a huge honour and privilege.

The occasion was made even more memorable for Drew as the Queen spoke personally to him at the end of the service.

Drew was able to tackle many new ventures during his time because as he recalls: 'New was good for a people who liked fresh ideas, being the descendants of frontier folk.' As a consequence, he initiated a Music Festival and music making with period instruments. He worked very successfully too with modern Kiwi composers to sing new settings for the services, notably with David Hamilton. Drew and the cathedral choir made many appearances on the New Zealand equivalent of the BBC's Songs of Praise programme, entitled Praise Be, still broadcast today by TVNZ and still occasionally showing the old clip or still photo from those days.

When this happens, Drew usually receives a screenshot sent by former members of the choir, several of whom went on to professional careers in music.

One of the things that struck Drew about life in New Zealand was its strong Maori culture. Their word 'whanau', pronounced 'farnow', showed him the importance of networks. The original Maori meaning was 'extended family.' The underlying importance to all New Zealanders of their extended responsibilities was a definite feature of the way in which the cathedral and the musicians conducted themselves.

St Paul's Cathedral, Buffalo

Christmas wherever it is celebrated is a highlight in the calendar and a busy one for musicians. In a southern hemisphere cathedral the choir would be singing the carol *Once in Royal David's City*, while outside the sun is burning down and the temperature rising to tropical levels. A barbecue would follow the Christmas morning service, at which the choir would certainly have worn summer gear under their cassocks. The barbecue signalled the beginning of their summer holiday.

After working in Wellington for five years, Drew left for pastures new. He was appointed as organist and choirmaster at St Paul's Cathedral, Buffalo, in upstate New York. This Episcopal cathedral has a long history, having been started in 1807, which makes it one of the earliest to be established in America. Its wonderful architecture marks it out as being a particularly significant building in the early history of the new country.

The city of Buffalo is also famed for having the largest domestic compound designed by the famous American architect, Frank Lloyd Wright, and is notable for having the country's first skyscraper. Once a part of an affluent and prosperous area, Buffalo has struggled economically in the past and that part of the States has been referred to as the Rust Belt. Thankfully, in recent years the second largest city in New York State has enjoyed a new lease of life.

In religious terms, Buffalo is largely a Roman Catholic city and so St Paul's congregation could be seen as a minority in the area.

Drew was appointed to create a choir sound along traditional Anglican lines to build on the traditional choir of men and boys which they had in place for over a hundred years. Both Drew and the cathedral came to realise that the Anglican choral tradition they wanted didn't always export so well and would be a challenge to achieve.

On his arrival, Drew found a boys' choir with just six or seven singers. However, he was told by the cathedral that an itinerary for a European tour had already been booked, eighteen months ahead, and that as everything was organised and paid for, it would be going ahead. That was certainly a huge test. In assessing his young singers, Drew quickly realised that a change of culture was necessary if he was to achieve the standard of singing which was required. The emphasis on how boys joined the choir needed to be shifted from a focus on outreach to one based more on musical ability. This therefore required the cathedral to offer musical education to the choristers, to support and monitor their development and improvement.

Although America prides itself on its religious freedom and tolerance, it was almost impossible for Drew to visit local schools and encourage boys to audition because of the fiercely secular nature of the educational system. Despite these challenges, Drew set about his task with his customary energy and drive. Also inheriting a girls' choir, he quickly built a group that became capable of singing some of the most demanding choral music in the repertoire, including Tippett's canticles for St. John's Cambridge and Bach's Liturgical Cantatas. The girls' choir virtually recruited itself and its singers zoomed ahead.

This group, for whom singing with the men's voices was a first for the cathedral, went on to successfully tour England and Sweden in 2007 and provided Drew with some exceptional performances.

The boys' choir continued to develop. When the time came for its European tour, the boys set off with their first stop being to sing Evensong at Exeter Cathedral. From this rather hesitant start, the choir moved onto Normandy and finally onto Paris where they were to sing Mass at Notre Dame Cathedral. Drew remembers the standing ovation they received from the final tour service as a true mark of how far that group of singers had come. The cathedral's generous budget had been well spent.

Buffalo is also well-known for its Albright-Knox Gallery, a 150-year-old institution with one of the world's finest art collections, including works by Van Gogh, Matisse, Warhol and Pollock. Drew well remembers the atmospheric annual Christmas concerts and services in the gallery's main atrium, and marvelling at the priceless art that acted as a backdrop to the music making. Kleinhans Music Hall on Symphony Circle, and Arts and Craft churches featuring countless architectural treasures, including windows by Tiffany, were other extraordinary venues for concerts and services. The Buffalo Philharmonic was a regular partner, as was the classical radio station WNED. One memorable evening involved girl and boy choristers being stuffed into a box at Tonawanda's Riviera Theatre, to sing the chorus parts of the Nutcracker Suite, played by the Philharmonic.

Then, in 2008 Drew returned to the UK to become organist and Master of the Choristers here at Croydon Minster, a post he held for four years. Nowadays, Drew is organist at The Royal Hospital School in Holbrook, Suffolk. He combines this with directing the Phoenix Singers, Framlingham, continuing the organ recitals for which he is in demand worldwide as well as other educational and examining roles. It is a wide and varied pot pourri of activities that Drew thoroughly enjoys.

It's not clear how many of those who saw or heard him during his tenure as choirmaster in Croydon quite understood the celebrity who was amongst us, and Drew's unassuming nature probably served to keep it that way. But learning about it has certainly enhanced my enthusiasm for the music of The Lord of the Rings.

A staccato Note about Charles Smith

Charles was the organist at Croydon Minster for a brief time in the early 1800s. He was born in Jermyn Street, London, in 1786. His father, Felton Smith, had been a chorister at Christ Church, Oxford. On showing very early musical promise he was pushed, especially by his mother, into being a musical protégé and began to play the piano by ear from a very early age. At five, he was given singing lessons by Thomas Costellow, showing that it is never too young to start.

His parents invited the great Dr Arnold to hear him sing and play. As a result of this soiree, Arnold advised Mr and Mrs Smith to send their son to the Chapel Royal, then under the leadership of Edmund Ayrton. By this time, though, Ayrton was already an old man and Charles left the Chapel Royal after just two years because Ayrton was unable to teach him properly. He was then placed under the tutelage of one John Ashley.

When he was just 13, Charles began singing at private parties and a year later in 1800 he sang at Ranelagh on the South Bank in vocal concerts and in their oratorios. As a young up-and-coming singer he became quite a favourite of the society ladies there and was invited to sing in Edinburgh and Glasgow, as well as in and around London.

His voice broke in 1803 at the age of 17. (We would consider that very late today). He therefore 'retired' to spend his time playing the organ and teaching.

Next came his fleeting appointment to Croydon. He was acting as deputy organist at the Chapel Royal when he appointed to the post of deputy organist in Croydon Minster.

Whether or not he was happy in Croydon we do not know, since in either case he did not stay long. Around 1806, against his parents' wishes, he travelled to Ireland to be an accompanist for a singer and her husband. Although he did return home briefly, he soon went back over to Dublin where he lived for about ten months. The reasons given for this stay have not been written down. In 1807 there is a note in the Irish Music Society's records which states that Charles was proposed for membership and admitted on April 7 of that year. When he did return to London, he took an organ job at Welbeck Chapel in Westmoreland Street, London.

It was now that a different stage of his musical career emerged. He had long been composing, but in 1808 his songs written for the show Yes or No were heard on the London stage when this show opened at the Haymarket Theatre on August 31st of that year. Although I have described it as a show, it would perhaps be more correct to call it an opera in English. Charles went on to have several successes over the next few years with shows such as Knapshou in 1809 and Hit or Miss which opened at the Lyceum in 1810.

His voice settled into a bass register and he sang in many oratorios, taking over singing appointments when James Bartleman became unwell towards the end of his career. Charles seemed to specialise in taking over from the great man. However, a musical dictionary of the day wrote that although his voice was rich, it was not powerful enough for a large theatre and in 1816 he left the stage.

He had married in 1815, a Miss Booth from Norwich who was also a musician, having been organist at the Octagon Unitarian Chapel in Norwich from 1809 and well-known in musical circles in the area. Music must have been to the fore in their household! In the newspaper announcement of the wedding, Charles' address is given as Westmoreland Road, Devonshire Place, London. Shortly after this, he gained a post described as 'lucrative' in Liverpool. And Charles' transfer to Liverpool was indeed very successful. The main musical compositions he wrote there, apart from some piano music, were his ballads with two titles being Far o'er the sea and The Battle of Hoenlinden. These were published by Power in the Strand. A well-known singer of the day, Miss Salmon, had great success with the first of these two titles.

The Harmonicom, a musical periodical of the time, wrote in 1824 that Charles composed 'some excellent English songs, publicly performed with great applause.' Both the audience and critics alike seemed to appreciate Charles' music. Another music periodical at the time is very critical about a composer who also set The Battle of Hoenlinden to music. It writes that the composer could not have listened to Charles Smith's tune, for if he had he would have realised how inferior his own efforts were!

Worse still, it goes on to say that this new work was a failure. Critics were clearly just as tough in Victorian times, although Charles on this occasion came off in a glowing light. Indeed throughout his career many people complimented him, including in his younger days, Samuel Wesley, who thought much of his organ playing.

Charles retired to Crediton in Devon and died there on 22 November 1856, having spent only a fraction of his life in Croydon. We have no record of any service at which he played but we do know from the comments of others about the prestigious talents with which he must have coaxed some sublime sounds from the Avery organ even in his teenage years.

Did you know...

Female voices have been part of the worship at Croydon Minster since the 1960's. The Girls' Choir was founded in 1966 by Christine Phillis who was a well known name both within the Royal School of Church Music as well as in church music circles as a whole. She ran the Girls' Choir for over thirty years before she stepped down in 1998. Her legacy still lives on today with the continuation of the Girls' Choir.

A sustained Note about F. Rowland Tims

Tims was organist of Croydon Minster from 1911 - 1918, then went on to a rather different sort of success, entertaining the public in the West End of London with his playing.

F. Rowland Tims, 1887-1956, the F standing for Frederick, began his musical career as a chorister at the cathedral of his hometown of Truro, Cornwall. He became an articled organ pupil there and eventually assistant organist, a post he held from 1902 to 1907. By this time he also held a Fellowship of the Royal College of Organists.

Moving from the far south west of England to Surrey, he next became organist first of Horsham Parish Church and second of Croydon Parish Church. He lived in Croydon from 1911 to 1918, and his name can be seen recorded on the church's organists' board.

A short time after leaving Croydon, in 1923, he became a concert organist, touring theatres with a large transportable Hill, Norman and Beard pipe organ. This instrument formed the centrepiece of a concert party of singers, instrumentalists and dancers billed as Vaudeville's Greatest Attraction - The Musical Romance.

The programme was based on the classics and light classics that were to be heard in the 'higher-class' cinemas of the day and it is thought that his signature tune, the Prelude to Act 3 of Richard Wagner's Lohengrin, may have been part of the introductory music to this show.

Regent Cinema, Brighton

In 1925 he entered the cinema world with a short spell at the Hill, Norman and Beard 'orchestral' organ of the Regent cinema, Brighton, moving next to a similar instrument at the new Capitol, later Gaumont, Haymarket, London. Silent film concert organs were going out of fashion following the introduction of theatre unit organs, but the Haymarket one, with a little up- dating, was accepted for broadcasting and recording. Tims cut his first tracks on it for HMV in 1928. Two of Tims' recorded songs were My song of the Nile and I'll see you again. It seems that he became quite attached to this instrument in the Haymarket, for when the 'talkies' (films with the modern addition of sound) arrived, he drew up a scheme for its rebuilding along modern lines.

In the mid 1930s, however, it was supplanted by a Compton organ. By all accounts this was a really good organ but for some reason HMV did not record with it and Tims's last recording sessions were on the superb Compton of the New Victoria, London. By this time the Great Depression had hit the country hard and he, like a number of other recording organists, was dropped from the recording companies' rosters.

Having enjoyed the prestigious position of Senior Professor at the British School of Cinema Organists from 1926 -1930, in April 1934 Tims moved to Union Cinemas as musical director, and went to Liverpool to play the large Compton in the new Paramount (later Odeon) theatre there. The Liverpool Echo reported that the Lord Mayor of Liverpool opened the building and Cecil B. DeMille's Cleopatra was the opening film. The article goes on to say that the cinema had hired the internationally renowned organist F. Rowland Tims and the price of an early bird ticket was one shilling. This description of him as an international organist shows the stature which he had by now attained in the musical world.

In 1937 he was to be found at the new Ritz, Birkenhead, where there was another large Compton organ. 4 October 1937 was its special first night, with Gracie Fields there to officially declare the cinema open. Tims played the organ which, 'had an illuminated console located on a lift in the centre of the orchestra pit.' Rising up from the pit must have given him a grand entrance!

Ritz Cinema, Birkenhead

This permanent position did not last long, though, and by the summer of 1938 he was freelancing. This, however, was to prove significant to his later career. From a guest engagement at the Regal (Odeon), St Peter's Port, Guernsey, he was flown direct to Aberdeen to play his first interlude at the Capitol that same night, 27 June 1938, with a presentation entitled Holiday Reminiscences. This performance was the beginning of a very successful twelve-year residency with the Capitol in Aberdeen.

In addition to his Capitol duties, he took up the post of organist first at Gilcomston South Church on Aberdeen's main street then, in 1946, at West St Andrew's (later Langstane Kirk) just a few doors down from the cinema.

He and his wife Violet moved into an upstairs flat which later became a hairdressing salon.

During the war years, Tims was kept busy running a highly successful scheme whereby members of the forces could write in with requests, the dedicatees of which were invited to come as special guests and hear the tunes played. He played a full part in the Aberdeen's musical activities, latterly becoming conductor of the Male Voice Choir of Hall Russell's shipyard. There were business activities as well. For a time during the war, he ran the Capitol's restaurant and at one point he and his wife also had a small cafe on the corner of Bath Street and Windmill Brae, not far from their flat.

'RT' left the Capitol in 1950 and in retirement concentrated on his choir work and other musical activities. He continued to teach individual pupils and remained a prominent figure in Aberdeen until his death from a stroke in 1956. You can still hear his playing today, as there is at least one track available on YouTube.

He was survived by many years by his widow Violet and their son Carl, who must have inherited his father's enthusiasms and for some time ran an organ studio in Stroud, Gloucestershire.

A staccato Note about James Harborough

It's impossible to know in exactly what ways James Harborough contributed to the life of Croydon and its church. He lies buried in its graveyard, and his gravestone shows that his contribution was musical. He's a brief, yet intriguing, musical Note in the Minster's history.

Walk round to the memorial garden outside the south door of the Minster to look at the line of gravestones standing by the path parallel to the wall of the church building and you will find one in memory of James Harborough. On the gravestone are carved two musical instruments: a bassoon and a horn. It suggests that in life, this man must have been a musician, either as a church player up in the gallery or perhaps in an orchestra or band in theatres and halls.

The words carved onto the stone, though now faint, tell us that James' father was named Thomas and was 'a tanner of this place.' Whilst the date is now illegible, the style of writing would indicate that the gravestone dates from the middle of the eighteenth century.

Who was this musician? Did he play here at the church? To give a little background, a top class bassoonist at that time could earn five shillings and ten pence nightly at Covent Garden. This would give a yearly income of £58 (based on a 220 night season). Unfortunately there is no evidence of where James might have played. Neither does James' name appear in the church's burial record.

If his father was a tanner, this provides a further line of enquiry. Looking beyond Croydon and into the surrounding areas, we discover a William Heath who owned and lived in Hall Place in Leigh-next-Tonbridge in the middle of the seventeenth century. This was a large house built in Tudor times, sitting on the banks of the River Cray in what we know today as Bexley. In William's employ, as a tanner, was one Thomas Harborough. Could this the man we are searching for?

It could be, but more proof would be needed. There are in fact several people with the surname Harborough in this area, with the earliest reference being to a John Harborough from Edenbridge who died in 1595.

He is described as a yeoman. There is also an entry for the baptism of James Harborough, son of Thomas Harborough at Chiddingstone, not far from Leigh, on 17 March 1764. Is this the man we are seeking? Another possibility is that James was not a player but rather a maker of instruments. As his father worked in leather, it could be that his son learned the skills of his trade and then went into making instruments.

But not all searches lead to a fruitful conclusion. Unfortunately on this occasion we are left without answers as to why a bassoon and a horn should decorate a gravestone by Croydon church. James Harborough strikes the softest and most fleeting of our staccato Notes, and certainly the hardest to hear clearly, but he is still a fascinating subject to speculate about.

Whoever he may have been, his musical interests clearly made enough of an impression on his contemporaries to be the way they decided to remember him. His contribution to the musical life of Croydon has been recorded and his bassoon and horn echo down the centuries to make us wonder.

Copyright British Institute of Organ Studies

A sustained Note about Frederick Cambridge

Frederick Cambridge was organist of Croydon Parish Church from 1868-1911, and has the distinction of being the longest holder of this position with a tenure of 43 years.

A look at the organists' board in Croydon Minster shows the list of position- holders from the date when the church was re-built after its destruction by fire (a dreadful event which took place in January 1867) to the present day. Some organists have spent a short time, while others have stayed longer. The longest serving organist is Frederick Cambridge, who was appointed to the position here in 1868, one year after the fire and just before the new building was re-dedicated. From the time of that appointment, Frederick stayed for 43 years, finishing his stint in 1911. That is an amazing amount of time to spend in his job here in the church, starting out as a young man of 27 and finishing when he was an old man of 70.

So what was the story of the man who devoted his working life to Croydon Minster?

He was born on 29 March 1841 in South Runton, Norfolk, just north of the town of Downham Market. He came from a farming family and Frederick is recorded in the 1841 census as living in Wiggenhall, South Runton.

The family made a good living from the land and in the 1861 census it states that the Cambridges owned 436 acres, employing 9 men and 8 boys. Frederick was not guided towards this life, however.

Instead he was sent to be a chorister at Norwich Cathedral, under Zechariah Buck, an often larger than life character who was in charge of the cathedral choir at the time. It is from this choral beginning that Frederick gained his interest in church music. Life was not all plain sailing for Frederick under Mr. Buck, though. As a cathedral articled pupil, he was one of 12 people from the cathedral choir playing the organ at different churches in the area. Frederick was responsible for the 3 nearby churches and occasionally played services at 8 or 10 others. Unfortunately, instead of receiving his small salary, the system was abused and it was Mr Buck who regularly pocketed the fees!

Frederick furthered his musical education by studying harmony with the German composer Wilhelm Molique, who was a contemporary of Ernst and Vieuxtemps. If these three names are unfamiliar then Baugniet's painting of the three of them, entitled Musical union, which hangs in the National Portrait gallery close to Trafalgar Square in central London may help. It was not until 1893 that Frederick was awarded a Bachelor of Music degree from Durham University.

Frederick began his paid organ duties at St. Columba's College, Rathfarnham, a suburb of Dublin, in 1862. Here he was responsible for the choir as well as his organ playing. He stayed until 1865 when he obtained his second position as organist at

St Mary's, Leicester. Here he stayed for two years until he started his job in Croydon.

As well as being the Minster's organist and choirmaster, Frederick became an important figure in the musical life of Croydon. He taught music privately and conducted the Croydon Vocal Union. He also organised and conducted Croydon church choir concerts. He was active in the Royal College of Music and served as its local examiner.

Frederick enjoyed composing and published many works in his lifetime. A variety of glees (a song often sung in three parts, popular in the late baroque, classical and early romantic periods), organ pieces and piano works are attributed to him. Alas, they have not stood the test of time. At the time, however, they were popular and before he arrived in Croydon, in 1863, Frederick had won the first prize of ten guineas in a competition to write the best glee organised by the Nottingham Anacreontic Society. Such societies were popular in the mid 19th century as clubs for amateur gentlemen musicians.

As a composer of church music, a communion service in C is attributed to him, along with a Te Deum and several anthems, of which two are noted in a biography of church composers: Not unto us, and I was in the Spirit. The Collection entitled Responses to the Commandments (1875) uses his service setting in C. Some hymns were also composed. In 1889 he published a hymn for Whit Sunday, beginning with the words 'Come, Holy Ghost...'. His Postlude in D is listed as the best of his organ compositions.

He certainly kept in touch with his Norfolk roots as his wife Lucy, whom he married in 1876, came from King's Lynn. She was five years younger than her husband. Their first child, Frederick Royston, was born later that year in Croydon. He was to grow up inheriting his father's musical genes as he is recorded in the 1911 census as being a violinist and a teacher of the violin.

That same 1911 census states that the Cambridge family was living in 1 Upper Coombe Street, Croydon, with two daughters, Lucy and Violet, and their son Frederick. What it doesn't tell us about is a terrible family tragedy.

Frederick's second son, John Cranmer Cambridge, drowned off the beach in Ostend at the age of only 23, trying to rescue a couple who had got into difficulties. The four Cambridge siblings were staying in the Belgian resort for their summer holiday at the Hotel Marion when on the very first day of their vacation, the two brothers responded to cries of help. The people in difficulty were, with help, pulled into a small boat, but when the other rescuers tried to reach John, he slipped beneath the waves. The date of the tragedy was 8 August 1901.

There is a plaque on the back wall of Croydon Minster dedicated to John, together with one in Postman's Park near to the Museum of London where there are several memorials to everyday heroes in the Victorian and early Edwardian times. John's loss must have been a terrible shock for all the Cambridge family and was something they had to live with for the rest of their lives.
The earlier 1901 census gives us a clue to the artistic talents of Frederick's wider family. Living with the family at that time was

Frederick's niece Sarah Birch. Forty-six years old and a spinster, her occupation is recorded as that of portrait painter. She had exhibited some paintings with the Ipswich Art Club but was never recognised as a major artist of her time. The census also names a young lady, Rosie Firth, as their maid, showing that the family had enough income to employ a servant.

Frederick ended his tenure of the Croydon church organist's job in 1911. It must have been an emotional farewell for him after serving as organist and choirmaster for so long. He died in Croydon on 17 December 1914, having appeared to have prospered and done very well there. Indeed he was well known enough to appear in a British Music Biography published in 1897, which includes musical artists, authors and composers of the day. Whatever the reasons for his remaining so long, I am sure he would look back on his longevity with some pride and sense of satisfaction, but always tinged by the tragedy of his son John.

Long Serving Choir Members

Organists and musical directors have long been dependent on the abilities and commitment of the members of their choirs. In our choir stalls there are a number of small memorial plaques remembering loyal and long serving choir members.

- William George Mills, nearly 40 years in the choir. Died 27 Feb 1947

- William Davis 1893-1958. 65 years service to this church and choir. Died 8 July 1961

- John William Puplett . 47 years of service, 20 as Hon Sec of the choir Died 8 Oct 1954

- William Henry Charles Hagger 1900-1965 45 years a member and bass soloist

- William Charles Lashwood 59 years a member of this choir. Died 7 Dec 1956

A staccato Note about John Rhodes

Some detective work with the national Census records has been necessary to tell the story of John Rhodes, another church organist, who travelled from the north of England to make a successful life for himself and his family in Croydon.

This note is not so brief as some, but has been only faintly recorded. It begins with a look at the 1861 national census return. It tells us that at 105 High Street in Croydon, in a dwelling named Harwood House, lived John Rhodes. His occupation is given as organist of Croydon Parish Church.

Further useful information to be found in that same census tells us that he was born in Westminster and that he was married to Frances. We can match this information from the 1861 census to the organist's board in Croydon Minster where it informs us that from 1857 to 1868, one John Rhodes was indeed the church's organist. The facts stated in the 1861 census are a starting point for us to find out more about him.

Using the details about where he was born, namely Westminster, a search in the 1851 Census of that area proved most interesting. At 39 King Street, Westminster, lived John Rhodes aged 60 and his wife Mary. The occupation stated for this John is fascinating in itself: he describes himself as a 'pianoforte maker and a tobacconist'. Not too many people ever describe themselves in those terms! Also living at that address is another John, their son, who is aged 18 and whose occupation is given as organist. Young John has three siblings living there too, the eldest of these, Selma, being as listed a milliner and dressmaker.

As we begin to build up the picture of our John, there are other snippets of information which help us further. John the father is listed as being born in Wakefield, Yorkshire, so at some point in his life a big decision was clearly made to come down to London. It is probably here where he met his wife Mary, as her birthplace is given as Bloomsbury, Middlesex. The family's Yorkshire roots can be traced further, as a John Rhodes is listed as a music seller in Darley Street, Bradford, in a book entitled The organ, its history and its construction. This was a vital resource for organ enthusiasts of the time. Published in 1855 and written by Hopkins and Rimbault, the substantial work informed music lovers of everything they needed to know about organs and organ playing and was partly funded by subscription. A list of its subscribers can be found in the book, with Prince Albert himself being the most prominent.

The story needs some further detective work at this point. If in 1851 our John is described as an organist, then we need to try to discover where he was playing, since he did not take the Croydon post until 1857. However, along with Prince Albert, another subscriber to Hopkin's and Rimbault's organ guide is one John Rhodes, described as the organist of St George The

Martyr, Southwark. We can reasonably deduce from this that John arrived in the organist's seat at Croydon straight from St George's, a little way to the north.

The organist's board at Croydon Minster then tells us that John completed his tenure here in 1868, so we also need to look for information about what happened to him and his family after that time. A search of the 1871 census for Croydon reveals that he and his wife were still living at 105 High Street. Life must have been treating them well as listed in their household is Mary-Ann Davis, a 'general domestic.' They now have five children, John 11, Frances 9, Alice 6, Cecil 4 and Montague 3. John's occupation is given as professor of music.

By the time the 1881 census was taken, the family was still resident in the High Street and its numbers had been increased by two, Edward, aged 8, and Ernest, 1. Their eldest son John, by now 21, is listed as an auctioneer's clerk, and the family still has a servant, this time named as Hagar King. In this 1881 census it tells us that John is 48 years old, making the year of his birth 1833 whilst his wife is 42, making her birth year 1839.

At this point our information trail runs cold, except for an announcement in the London Gazette which tells us that John died on 3 September 1885. What sort of man was he? Where was his musical career as a professor taking him? These are questions for a future search. For now, we have put together a fascinating story from the plain entry on the organists' board.

Did you know...

The singing of psalms has been a feature of church services here for hundreds of years. Every Sunday evening in term time the choir sings Choral Evensong. Included in that service will be the psalm which is appointed for that week. The current choir sing the psalms to a range of tunes and chants.

The Organist's Pocket Companion produced by John Johnson was a collection of the psalms and the tunes generally used in Parish Churches and chapels in London. Published towards the end of the 17th century it was printed for Johnson at the Harp and Crown at Cheapside. No Church House publishing in those days!

The Pocket Companion includes such psalm tunes as London Old, London New, St. David's and Martyr's. It also includes what Johnson describes as the "proper" tunes for a particular numbered psalm. Whilst there is no documentary evidence to say that any of these tunes were actually used in Croydon Parish Church, it would be safe to say that it would be highly likely that they were.

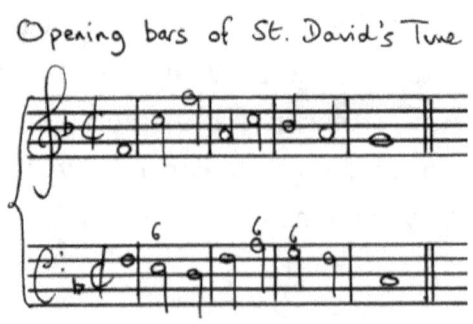

Opening bars of St. David's Tune

A sustained Note about H. Leslie Smith

Leslie Smith was the Minster's organist from 1918 to 1948 - and his note begins with a riddle. What connects freemasonry, musical conducting, a love of playing billiards and a nickname of 'Hoppy'? Intrigued? Then read on.

H. Leslie Smith was born in March 1870, the son of Charles Henry Smith and his wife Emma. A musical talent emerged early in his life and he was a solo chorister at St Saviour's Church in west Croydon when he was still a young boy. 'H' (Herbert) was educated at Whitgift School before he went on to attend the Royal College of Music, where he studied for six years.

Even before going to the Royal College, his musical education had benefited from the advice of his uncle Mr H. L. Balfour, one-time organist of the Royal Albert Hall. At the Royal College, Leslie studied under some of the most illustrious musicians of the day; Charles Villiers Stanford taught him composition, Sir Frederick Bridge harmony and counterpoint, John Francis Burnett pianoforte, Dr Gladstone organ and Dan Price singing.

Such a background in music made him the prime candidate who was chosen to be appointed to the position of organist and choirmaster at Croydon church at the end of the First World War.

When Whitgift School celebrated its tercentenary (300 years' anniversary) in 1896, Dr Haig-Brown, headmaster of Charterhouse School, composed a commemoration ode that was set to music by Leslie. Also in that year Leslie married Kathleen Russell, daughter of John Scott Russell of Croydon.

In 1899, Leslie started the St James' Philharmonic Society or the Croydon Sacred Harmonic Society, later the Croydon Philharmonic, with his uncle H.L. Balfour. He was its conductor for many years. At the end of the First World War, he wanted to take the lead in any peace celebrations in the borough and began rehearsals of Handel's Messiah straightaway. A report written in a local history publication tells us that there was a large choir and as large an orchestra as could be accommodated in the Parish Church.

The music was conducted by Mr Alan Kirby with Mr Leslie Smith accompanying on the organ. Leslie was very much involved in the musical life of Croydon. He conducted productions of the Croydon Stager's Operatic

Society, a fine example of which was Gilbert and Sullivan's Yeoman of the Guard at the Public Hall in 1912. He had commitments way beyond Croydon as well. In 1913 he was engaged to coach the chorus at London's Guildhall School of Music for the production of Edward German's Merrie England, and he was the musical director for a time of the Burgon Opera Recital Company, touring England and Scotland on many occasions.

In a musical 'who's who' of the day, Leslie listed his hobbies as tennis and billiards, and was also a keen freemason. In an archive we read that in May 1920 he was at a meeting of prospective founders of the Waddon Lodge, which was held in the local Greyhound Hotel. Full approval to begin the lodge was given later the same year. Its first Worshipful Master (head of the branch) was Brother Leslie. It was a temperance lodge, meaning that the consumption of alcohol was discouraged, but a special licence was granted for them to celebrate the opening! For the remainder of his life, freemasonry was an integral strand.

Further evidence of his teaching can be found in The Rise and Fall of a Musical Empire, a book about the work of impresarios Ibbs and Tillet, in which we read that a soprano named Lena Elbert was given a poor review for a show and it was suggested that she 'required further study with her teacher, H. Leslie Smith.' She would have been just one of the many individual pupils who benefitted from Leslie's skills as an outstanding accompanist.

Leslie composed a quantity of church music during his lifetime as well as numerous songs and orchestral works. None of these compositions have survived to be in any current repertoires, however. One example of his composition was his Jubilate Deo in D for unison voices and organ, which was published by Stainer and Bell in 1949.

We know that he lived at Lynton Holme, 32 Oakfield Road, Croydon. It therefore seems he was a real Croydon man, through and through. There is a reference to him in 1929 conducting the Central Croydon Music Society in a piece entitled Golden Fleece, and further evidence of his influence on the local music scene from the Musical Times of 1 November 1931. We read there that Leslie was one of the driving forces in running the Third Triennial

Croydon Festival during November of that year. The festival was based in the Parish Church and the Baths Hall, and began on the Sunday afternoon with a service conducted by Leslie Smith in the Parish Church. On Tuesday night at the Hall, Sir Edward Elgar was to conduct his Meditation from the Light of Life and the Dream of Gerontius.

A different strand of musical influence can be found in the latter years of his tenure at Croydon Parish Church. Embracing the growth of the new media, H. Leslie Smith's name appears regularly in the Radio Times magazine throughout the 1930s and 1940s when the Home Service, as it was called in those days, broadcast many services from Croydon Parish Church on the radio. On 6 October 1935 a celebration of harvest was broadcast, featuring tunes from the Ancient and Modern hymnbook and including the seasonal favourites, We plough the fields and scatter and Fair waved the golden corn. On 18 May 1947 he played the organ for an edition of a programme called Sunday Half Hour which consisted of hymn singing. It was broadcast on the Light Programme from Croydon church itself.

Leslie certainly made his mark in Croydon, remaining in his post here for 30 years. One chorister remembers that he was always known as 'Hoppy' and that he was a real stickler for discipline. His work both in the church and in the wider community was appreciated and acknowledged by everyone. After he had left his post in Croydon he remained committed to church music, becoming organist at Windsor parish church from 1962 until his death in 1973.

Croydon Parish Church Choir 1947

James Bartleman

A staccato Note about James Bartleman

James was a distinguished singer who was appointed organist at Croydon Parish Church from 1794 until 1804, making him the first professional to have played on the fine instrument built by John Avery.

The church here in Croydon, known either as the Parish Church or latterly as the Minster, has always been known for the high quality of its music. Many outstanding musicians have performed here, as well as holding the office of organist and choirmaster. This note concerns one of those outstanding musicians whose name was James Bartleman.

Bartleman was one of the leading bass soloists of his generation. He sung in the Chapel Royal and in the choir of Westminster Abbey. In fact, after his death he was held in such high regard that was remembered by a memorial stone placed in the cloisters of the Abbey itself.

In an edition of the periodical magazine Christian Remembrancer, published in 1834, there is a section about the history of cathedral and parochial church organs of this country. Number 17 in this series of articles was about the organ in Croydon.

This was the instrument, which was built by John Avery, the renowned organ builder of the late 18th and early 19th century, and completed in 1794.

The Christian Remembrancer tells us that this organ was in a better state of preservation than any of the other Avery organs in London. It then goes on to inform the reader that money was left by a parishioner to purchase this organ and that the first organist was 'Mr Bartleman, the late celebrated bass singer.'

As previously mentioned, one objection raised to the new organ was the issue of making payment to an organist, but this opposition was overcome and an annual voluntary subscription for the organist was agreed. Mr Bartleman's successors, too, were remunerated for their attendance by voluntary subscription.

If the organ was installed in 1794 and Bartleman was its first organist, the assumption is that is the date when he began his tenure in Croydon. This has not been proven though. What we do know about Bartleman, however, is very interesting.

Born in 1769 in Mortimer, near Reading in Berkshire, Bartleman's biggest musical influence seems to have been Dr Cooke, the organist and choirmaster at Westminster Abbey. It is said that Bartleman entered the Westminster choir at a young age and was celebrated as a boy chorister for his performance of Greene's anthem, 'Acquaint thyself with God.' When his voice broke and he settled into a bass baritone pitch, he became known for his outstanding performances of Purcell.

He was also known as a madrigal player and glee singer, being a founder member of the Glee Club. Whatever genre he sung, he was always said to bring the music alive with energy, singing with great clarity and expert enunciation. A letter written to a periodical after his death by one of his pupils, Miss Julia R. Bockett, explains that 'his pronunciation and articulation were beautiful.' She continues in her letter that 'she had never heard his like since.' It wasn't only former pupils who so admired him. The New Monthly magazine of the time wrote that Bartleman 'stood unrivalled in his profession as a bass, having a fine-toned melodious voice.' It would have been a real privilege to have heard him sing.

Bartleman began to sing professionally in 1788 when his name appears on concert bills of ancient music. In 1791 he left the performing group in which he began, and commenced his notable solo career. From 1792 to 1797 he sang in many oratorios in Covent Garden. The composers Calcott and Crotch both wrote songs especially for him.

He did return to the ancient music concerts after a few years, but suffered very poor health for many years before his death on 15 April 1821 in Berners Street, London. On his memorial stone, placed in the cloisters of Westminster Abbey very close to his mentor Dr Cooke, are etched the opening notes from an aria that he used to sing, by Pergolesi, 'O Lord, have mercy upon me.' About his organ playing we know nothing! We can only hope his playing was as good as his singing.

Just one reference remains and that says that after his resignation from his post at Croydon, his deputy Charles Smith took over. It states that Charles was about eighteen when he commenced

his duties as deputy. That would have been 1804, so this does provide us with the year that Bartleman resigned. So to this we can add knowledge of the second paid organist of the era after the installation of the Avery organ. Together with Thomas Miller, who played the organ here for no fee for many years, Bartleman and Smith made up the triumvirate who must have been responsible for much of the church's music from 1794 to well into the 19th century.

Of James Bartleman there is little else to tell. We know he had two sisters to whom he left his music collection. Unfortunately it seems that the auctioneer responsible for the sale of these goods to raise money was less than honest about what he passed onto the two ladies. Thus disappointment dogged not only the final years of his life, shadowed by a particularly debilitating illness, but also continued after his death.

The question remains for us, though. How well could he play that organ? When playing, he would have been seated high above the west end door as the organ was placed at that end of the church. There was a gallery where the choir would have sung. I feel sure that however well he may have played the organ, his first love would always have been the voice.

A sustained Note about John Avery

John Avery built the organ in the original Croydon Parish Church in 1794. 73 years later it was destroyed when the building burned to the ground on the night of 5 January 1867.

Local churchwardens and the clergy in the early 1790s were faced with an interesting situation. Croydon Parish Church, as our Minster was called in those days, had been left a significant amount of money by a gentleman named Christopher Burrell, a bell ringer in the tower. In his will he stipulated that the money was to be used for the construction of a pipe organ.

Given its important position as one of the most significant parish churches in Surrey as well as the areas around London, due to its links with the Archbishop of Canterbury, any decision about a new organ would have to be carefully made. We know nothing of the deliberations about the new instrument. The only recorded comment seems to be that some folk were against it since it would mean having to pay an organist a salary!

But the decision to build a new organ was taken, and the person appointed to do so was John Avery, who lived in Westminster. He was one of the leading organ builders of his day and had already completed some significant contracts, namely in Cornwall at St

Michael's Mount parish church and in nearby Kingston-upon-Thames, a task he completed immediately before taking on the Croydon contract. After completing the task, he took on even more eminent projects, completing some very well known organs in King's College Cambridge and at St Margaret's Westminster.

As in today's world, it took time to become professionally established and much of any business relied on word of mouth. This worked against Avery on one occasion when a gentleman named Marsh was telling a friend that he was looking to install an organ in his house and was thinking of using John Avery to carry out the job. The friend 'gave rather an indifferent character of him (Avery)' and recommended Hancock of Wyche Street who he said was a very good workman and long established. Unlike today, there were many people working in the organ building trade back then.

It takes a particular set of skills to design and build a huge pipe organ. As someone whose DIY skills falter when asked to saw a piece of wood in half, I can only marvel at the way in which Avery not only had the practical skills, but also the visionary expertise to create the mechanisms which would lead to glorious sounds. When Croydon's organ was finished in 1794, it was considered to be one of Avery's finest achievements.

In a church building which was described as 'favourable to sound', he set to work. He was accomplished in creating instruments that could use a variety of stops to create different sounds. One commentator describes the Croydon organ as having 'a generous provision of mixtures, cornets and reeds in the eighteenth century manner.' The tone of the instrument was said to be rich and powerful with Avery's signature qualities clearly heard, these being 'a brilliance in the chorus and a quickness in speech.' In layman's terms, Avery seemed to be able to produce an organ with a rich and vibrant tone, which forms its broad musical 'brush strokes', and also upon which the organist can easily run over the keys to produce a solo line in a variety of instrumental sounds, forming the detailed 'painting'.

Building an organ is a slow and lengthy process. One business concern on such a project would be cash flow. An integral part of modern day contracts would incorporate certain dates for payments as the project progressed, so that the contractor could properly plan for the buying of materials and the paying of wages. But it seems Avery found the economic side of the business difficult to manage: he was declared bankrupt on three separate occasions during his life.

The first of these was recorded in the London Gazette on 18 November 1775. His address was given as St George's in Bloomsbury. On the second occasion, dated 14 Dec 1790, he was described as a 'musical-instrument maker'. The third time is dated 8 Dec 1801 and he is again described as an organ maker. Sadly, when he died in 1806, he was being held in Giltspur Street compter. A 'compter' is a word for a small prison, usually for holding debtors. This particular one was in Smithfield, London, close to Newgate gaol. Opened in 1791, it was only in operation until 1853. Avery never lived to see the completion of the project he was engaged in at the time of his death, namely the building of a new organ for Carlisle cathedral.

We are able build up a better picture of John Avery and his trade through a surprising source: the Old Bailey archives. There it states that one Joseph Robson was indicted for 'feloniously stealing, on 1 August 1797, a wainscot board, value 3s, a lignum vitae tool, value 2s, two gouge bits, value 1s, one reed bit, value 3s, a steel reed mandrit, value 3s, a burning iron, value 1s, a trumpet reed and tongue, with block and socket, value 3s, thirty pipe mandrils, value 10s, two chissels, value 2s, and two mahogany mouldings, value 1s, the property of John Avery.'

When John Avery takes the witness stand, he confirms his name and his occupation as organ builder. He explains that about a year ago some tools of his had gone missing. He says he had just returned from working in the country in July 1797, but unfortunately does not say where this was. His account goes on to reveal that others who worked for him had said that the defendant was unreliable and that he had indeed taken some of Avery's tools. Avery and Robson had had an altercation on a working site where blows and insults were exchanged, and Avery later went to the police to seek a search warrant to search Robson's lodgings in Little George Street.

Reluctant at first to let the constable in, Robson nevertheless allowed the search to take place and Avery went through his things identifying tools and the wainscot board which he said were his. Under cross-examination, Avery was asked whether Robson was an ingenious fellow. Avery replied that he was, that he was a useful worker and that he had trained him so. Robson was described as a journeyman tradesman. Avery said that the tools that were taken were those that were needed to make, as he says, 'the work.' Surprisingly, Avery goes on to say that the only tools that were needed when they went out to the site where the organ was being erected were screwdrivers and pincers for installation, the rest of this complex construction task having already been completed.

In his defence, Robson then says that workers often took tools home to finish pieces of work. He said he could prove that the wooden board was one he purchased from a timber merchant in Little St Martin's Lane. Robson also states that he thought Avery was jealous of him because he was setting up in his own business as an organ builder. He also adds that not six weeks before the events described took place, Avery had been arrested for being in debt and allowed Robson to complete sections for the organs they were building in Whitehall and at Mr White's the auctioneers at Storey's Gate. (In an age of growing affluence, many well to do folk were having organs installed in their homes). Avery had a long history of building such smaller organs. One that he built in 1779 eventually found its way to New Zealand. It was eventually installed there in Ponsonby Baptist church, which paid £98 for it in 1898.

This custom of lending tools to workman was supported in court by three other organ builders, John Preston, John Wright and Thomas Gibson. Six other witnesses were called to give Robson a good character report and at the end of the trial he was found not guilty. Avery would not have been pleased with this verdict. However, this was not the first time that Avery had accused someone of a crime who had then been found not guilty. Earlier that same year he had accused Henry Gray of stealing a linen handkerchief of his, valued at one shilling. This time Gray was found not guilty because the court said that Avery had acted hastily. Gray may well have been in the act of stealing but hadn't actually done it when apprehended by Avery.

One could conclude that Avery was not a great judge of others' characters or that he was prone to acting aggressively or hastily to his own detriment. Put this information together with the notes found in several historical sources that Avery was very partial to a drink and was in fact often drunk, and we have a picture of a man who was able to make exquisite organs that produced sounds of the very highest quality but who found other areas of his life a real challenge.

The organ he built in Croydon church was constructed at the west end, above where the main entrance is today. It had a total of 1653 pipes. All were in agreement that this was one of, if not the very best of, all Avery's completed projects. His skills and talents were shared though, as one of his apprentices, Alexander Buckingham, went on to work for another well- known organ maker, Thomas Elliott, before branching out on his own.

I think the clergy and churchwardens of Croydon would have been pleased with the outcome of their new organ project, but saddened to hear later of the difficulties of a talented but flawed individual.

Organ Specifications for the 1794 Avery Organ

For the benefit of readers who wish to know about the technical aspects organs in our church, here is the specification of the 1794 Avery organ. The details for this have been taken from the Organa Britannica publication which used Sperling's notebooks as their main source material. John Hansen Sperling was a member of the Church of England clergy who took a particular interest in church organs. He was admitted to Trinity College Cambridge in January 1843, matriculating with a BA in 1848 and ordained Curate the following year. He was curate at St Mary Abbotts Kensington, located on Kensington High Street, until 1856. He appeared to keep his organ notebooks until 1854. We do not know why he stopped compiling them, except to say this was the year he got married! It is from his notebook that we find the Avery organ of St John the Baptist, the then Parish Church of Croydon, containing some 1671 pipes.

From this number of pipes we can quickly see and understand that it was a organ of great size and complexity. The total number of pipes is made up as follows; 904 in the Great organ, 453 in the Choir, 296 in the Swell together with 17 Pedals. There were four couplers. When the organ was originally constructed there was a Pedal section whose few pipes met an incomplete Great Open Diapason.

In 1817 the instrument was modified by Thomas Eliott, one of the leading organ builders and repairers of the day, who put all those pipes onto the Great console and supplied an octave and a half of large unison open Pedal Pipes.

Sperling outlines the specifications of Avery's organ in the following way;

Great organ and Choir GG to F in alt
Swell 3 octaves tenor F to F in alt,
One and a half octaves of Pedal Pipes.

Great	**Swell**	**Choir**
Open Diapason Front Pipes	Open Diapason	Stopped Diapason
Open Diapason	Stopped Diapason	Dulciana
Stopped Diapason	Principal	Principal
Principal	Cornet 3 ranks	Flute
Flute	Trumpet	Fifteenth
Twelfth	Hautboy	Cremona
Fifteenth		Furniture 2 ranks
Sex: 3 ranks		
Mixture 3 ranks		
Trumpet		
Mounted Cornet to C 5 ranks		
Pedal Pipes to GGG.		

A staccato note about boy soprano Leslie Tasker.

Leslie Tasker was a chorister who joined the choir in 1944. However angelic they may appear, his story reveals that the church's young choristers got up to a considerable amount of mischief!

Just imagine for a moment what it might be like in the choir vestry, when boy choristers become embroiled in an argument and start throwing hymnbooks at each other. You can almost hear the shrieks piercing the air. You can visualise the mess on the floor. Then the door opens and in comes the choirmaster. With sharp words and clear, stern instructions, the high jinks are over and order is restored. But what should be done with the choirboys now?

Leslie Tasker's memories of being a chorister here at Croydon included such an incident. The decorum of the choir vestry was so shattered, he recalls, that all of the choristers were suspended for three weeks!

It was left to the men of the choir to sing the services in the meantime, until the suspension was complete and the boys were reinstated.

We can assume too that there were many parental admonishments and it would have been a chastened group who met again for their 4.30pm Monday practice as they resumed their singing duties.

Joining the choir as an 8 year old in 1944, Leslie was following in the footsteps of his brother and three cousins who were already members. Leslie was the 35th boy and was at the bottom of the pile. No auditions were needed to become a chorister, but anyone who couldn't keep the correct pitch or who had trouble learning the melodies would eventually be asked to leave. All the choir boys had the opportunity of taking the Royal School of Church Music level 1 award which helped them to develop their singing skills as well as their musical knowledge and awareness. The ordering of the choristers was very similar to the positioning of pupils in a junior school classroom when I was a youngster, where sitting in single file row order, your position was determined by regular testing in Maths and English. In the choir, your positioning was similarly determined by how well each boy was singing. In practices much of the time was given over to singing psalms. The first verse would be sung by the 1st boy, the second by the 2nd boy and so on. If a chorister made a mistake and sung his section poorly, he would be asked to swop their position with the boy one below him. That definitely added competition to proceedings.

As well as singing psalms, the choristers have to sing at least two anthems every week. Over time, they developed a very wide repertoire.

The man in charge of the choir then was Leslie Smith, a leading freemason of the local area.

A quiet man, the attention of the choristers in the choir stalls would be gained by Smith tapping his wedding ring on the top of a wooden pew. Although he would conduct and lead the choir from the front in rehearsals, he would just play the organ for church services, leaving the choristers to start singing by listening to the introduction and counting for the correct number of beats without a conductor to encourage and remind them of exactly how they should be singing. The choristers had to sing two services each Sunday. At 11 am there was a service of Choral Matins. At 6.30pm there was Choral Evensong. Back in the 1940s, the church would have been full for each of these services.

The choir in those days was large, consisting of 35 boys and around 30 men. Choristers were not paid to sing on a Sunday but they did get paid two shillings for each wedding and back then there were many of them. What a treat it would have been to arrive home at the end of a busy Saturday with a 10 shilling note in your pocket having sung at five wedding services. This was the maximum number on any one day that Leslie recalls.

Weddings can be a source of many stories and memories. There was the occasion when 10 choristers turned up to a fifteen minute rehearsal before a wedding service but one subsequently went missing. Choirmaster Leslie Smith was perplexed as to why only nine of them processed into the church to begin the service. Choir vestry high jinks had again broken out! One boy's cap had been thrown up onto the organ casement in the vestry. The lad concerned had put a stepladder against the wooden casing and climbed up to fetch his headwear - only for other choristers to think it hilarious to take the ladder away and leave him stranded on the high flat surface during the ceremony. Graciously the culprits got the ladder out again after the wedding ceremony had finished and the lad could get back down!

Many folk are nervous about weddings, none more at times than the bride's father. During one service when the married couple moved to the High Altar for the blessing, the man pulled out a hip flask to take a refreshing swig. Realising he was being closely observed by the choir, he turned to the nearest chorister and offered the flask to him, too! Leslie refused.

Having already mentioned two instances of high jinks with the choristers, you can imagine that there would be others. Indeed there were, but as part of this chorister's tale we need to understand what happened to each chorister when they first joined the choir. Initiation ceremonies to a lesser or greater extent have been a part of many institutions, whether one agrees with them or not. Back in 1944, this is what awaited all the newcomers. At the rear of the church, in the corner of the area now known as the Garden of Remembrance, was a pit. This was where vegetation was thrown after the tidying of the church grounds as well as decayed floral displays from the church.

It was into this pit that new entrants to the choir were thrown. Leslie remembers that the pit was deep enough so that small boys could not climb out without assistance. Some were left in the pit for the whole hour of the rehearsal.

In case you are wondering what would happen when the pit was full of vegetation, as it would be on occasion, there's a simple answer: you were taken and swung into the holly bush by the side of the church building! But such ceremonies did not put off the boys and the number of applicants wishing to join continued to be high.

Given the high jinks already outlined in this tale, I hardly dare state the final incident which Leslie remembers. This was an occasion when choirboys chased a curate up on the North Aisle roof, found a hose left over from the war with a water supply still attached and sprayed him with it! These stories could be the basis of a new film, 'Carry On Chorister.' However, the old adage of playing hard and working hard was appropriate here, as despite these incidents, the music the choir produced was of a very high standard. You can imagine the older officious male singers looking down their noses at any young chorister who did not toe the line when in a service.

Attitudes to safety and supervision were very different back in the 1940s. Today no chorister leaves a service or a practice without the choirmaster or the choir matron knowing and checking who is to collect them.

Back then, Leslie and his friends would run off home with no thought of supervision. A spare length of string in the pocket was ideal to tie two neighbouring front door knockers together on the way home. Did they ever stop playing tricks!

Just as being a chorister requires commitment today, so too the chorister from the 1940s had to give up a great deal of time to the cause. Each boy was required to attend practice three times every week. On Mondays and Wednesdays the rehearsals were from 4.30pm to 5.30pm. On Fridays the boys rehearsed on their own from 7pm until 8pm, when there were joined by the men and continued until 9 pm. The men of the choir all came from the local area, working mainly in banks, shops and local businesses. Soloists were chosen from this group and the standard of singing was very high.

Late 19th century music, including such notable composers as Stainer and Stanford, was the main repertoire of the choir. Indeed, Stainer's Crucifixion was the annual Good Friday musical offering. When Leslie sang in the choir there was no such thing as the term times which we have today. The choir sang for 52 weeks a year, with the boys being allowed the odd week or two off in the summer for family holidays. There were of course treats! One of them was going to Gilbert's bakers over the road to get a Nelson's slice. This was a traditional slice of bread pudding which the choristers would often buy before they went into the rehearsals.

The choristers also enjoyed much camaraderie and friendship. The vast majority of the younger boys attended the Parish Church School, now the Minster School, and could enjoy football and cricket matches on a Saturday, usually against local schools such as Royal Russell. At Christmas time they could look forward to treats of mince pies when they went to sing carols for various local dignitaries in their houses along Park Hill.

As the boys grew up together in the choir, church activities became a way of life for them. One interruption in their singing would be for a short time as their voices broke. After a few weeks' rest, they would return to sing in the range their new voice would allow. The only enforced break for the young men was when they went off for their National Service. In their mid teens, as well as staying in the choir, many also became part of the Young Communicants' Club and would attend the 8am Communion Service together. In addition, they would put on three or four shows a year with music, monologues and short sketches which they would write themselves.

In those days, very few choristers would go off to university so there would be much more continuity than there is today. Indeed, the YCC became a local marriage bureau!

Croydon Minster has a long and distinguished history of choral singing. Leslie has been a part of that history. For those of you who have never been, do come and listen to the choristers of today as they continue this legacy. Individual tales might end but the story is still being written and the music continues.

A sustained Note about John Pyke Hullah

A fine musician and collaborator with the novelist Charles Dickens, John was Croydon's church organist from 1837-1858.

The list of organists who have held the position here at Croydon Minster contains many eminent musicians and teachers. But I wonder if you knew that one of our organists wrote a comic opera entitled 'The Village Cocquettes.' Not only that, but he did so in collaboration with none other than the eminent novelist Charles Dickens, who wrote the libretto.

Described as an 'operatic burletta', the work was first performed at the St James Theatre in London on 5 December 1836. It didn't achieve great critical acclaim and closed after seventeen nights, although it was revived again in April 1837, this time lasting for 27 performances before finishing on 17 May. The composer's name was John Pyke Hullah, who in that same year of 1837 was appointed to the organist's post here in Croydon.

Dickens and Hullah first started to discuss writing a light opera together in December 1835. Originally the idea for the opera came from Hullah who suggested it be based around an Italian idea and featuring a gondolier.

Dickens preferred an English story which centred on characters who could act and talk in a way that the audience might be familiar with in this country, and so an historical romance took shape.

Dickens' story was published separately in book form between the two theatre runs. Hullah's tunes were also published but the majority of the music was lost in a fire in December 1836 in a house in Edinburgh belonging to the music librarian of the Theatre Royal there, where the opera had also been performed. In order to provide a tiny flavour of the opera, the following two verses are taken from the opening chorus of labourers set in a 'rick-yard with a cart laden with corn-sheaves.'

> Hail to the merry Autumn days, when
> yellow cornfields shine,
> Far brighter than the costly cup that holds
> the monarch's wine!
> Hail to the merry harvest time, the gayest of the year,
> The time of rich and bounteous crops, rejoicing,
> and good cheer!
> 'Tis pleasant on a fine Spring morn to see the buds
> expand, 'Tis pleasant in the Summer time to view
> the teeming land;
> 'Tis pleasant on a Winter's night to crouch around the
> blaze, — But what are joys like these, my boys,
> to Autumn's merry days!

A review of the opera in the Theatrical Examiner was very harsh. 'Mr Hullah is, we understand, a young gentleman from the Royal Academy. We think he has completely mistaken the genre of

English music. We must conceive it to be an error to set English words to music after the manner of any foreign school.' Hullah's only consolation may have been that virtually everything else about the production received equally harsh criticism.

Putting that experience behind him, Hullah arrived in Croydon and seemed to enjoy his time here. From the notes in his own diary he writes that the original church dates from the 14th century and is a 'noble and interesting one.' He goes on to write that it contained 'an organ by Avery, a builder of considerable repute, and though old-fashioned in its keyboard, of great sweetness and beauty'. Hullah lived in Croydon in lodgings in a house owned by Thomas Miller, a gentleman whom he described as being of 'high culture' and who will appear again in this publication in a Note of his own.

At this time, despite the additional demands of his organist's post, Hullah continued to compose and on 11 November 1837 his opera, 'The Barbers of Bassora' opened at Covent Garden. This was a comic opera in two acts. This time, he collaborated with Madison Morton who wrote the libretto. The following year, on 17 May, a second opera opened, called 'The Outpost'. Unfortunately neither of these operas was successful and these proved to be his final foray into this musical genre.

John was born in Worcester on 27 June 1812. It is said he got his musical talent from his mother. He began his time at the Royal Academy of Music in 1833 and was taught singing by Domenico Crivelli. It was two years later when he met Dickens' sister, Fanny who was also studying under Crivelli.

Thus began their partnership leading to the production of their light opera.

After his unsuccessful forays in musical theatre, John turned his attention to teaching singing and developed into one of the most influential figures in the Victorian musical world. After a visit to Paris to study the methods and systems used by Joseph Mainzer, Hullah returned to England determined to bring singing to the masses. Supported by the Prime Minister Lord Melbourne and by Professor James Key, in effect the Education Secretary of the day, he began classes to teach both singers and tutors, so much so that by 1841 it was estimated that 50,000 working class children were learning singing from teachers taught by Hullah.

It was in 1841 that the Church of England began its first teacher-training centre in St Mark's Chelsea. Choral singing was placed at the heart of the curriculum. What a joy it is to read that sentence! Hullah was engaged to lead and develop this project. In 1872 he was appointed as National Inspector of Music and kept this position for ten years before being succeeded by John Stainer. For many years he conducted a concert at the Crystal Palace of the Children of the Metropolitan Schools.

John left his Croydon post in 1858 when he went to become the organist at Charterhouse School, where he had held a regular singing class. He stayed in this post until his death on 21 Feb 1884, at his home in Grosvenor Mansions, Victoria Street, Westminster.
He is buried in Kensal Green cemetery in west London.

During his lifetime he wrote a vast amount of music, as well as several books, especially about how to teach singing. At St. Martin's Hall he arranged and conducted many concerts. A poster from 1858 advertises the first concert of the season on Wednesday 17 November at 7.30pm, with John Hullah in St. Martin's Hall, Long Acre, London. This hall was opened through the generosity of his supporters and backers and he continued to perform there until it burnt down in 1860. After this, Hullah was forced to gain income in as many ways as possible and he was engaged to give a series of lectures on the history of modern music at the Royal Institute in early 1861.

Hullah wrote a number of hymn tunes which can still be found in hymnbooks today. 'O Word Of God Incarnate' is sung to his tune, Bentley and other hymn tunes of his include Sellinge, St. Bruno and St Isidore.

He was indeed a national figure, but in the years before his fame he spent his time in Croydon properly training the choir and introducing tunes with strong melodies to replace the tunes favoured by church gallery musicians. One can only wonder how his early singing teaching went. He must have possessed a real gift for it. Was he a Gareth Malone of his day, able to inspire and motivate singers of all types and background? It would be good to think so.

A staccato Note about Frederick Kill Harford.

Frederick was a pioneering advocate of the belief, now widely accepted, that music has therapeutic value.

What is your favourite piece of music? Is it the one that you have enjoyed for many years or have you recently encountered something new? Of course, your answer can depend on your mood. Music has the ability to raise the spirit, soothe a troubled mind and, indeed, invoke many memories. Some people use the calming of music to settle them into a night's slumbers. We might disagree with each other's choices but for the vast majority of us, music is an integral and important part of our lives.

This is never more true than when we are feeling under the weather, for music has the potential to lift us. And over the last hundred years, music has played an increasingly important role in helping the healing process. It is widely acknowledged by professionals that music can help to bring you out of a dark place. It can also give great comfort to patients suffering from dementia and their families, for people who have lost much of their ability to recall recent events can be stimulated to remember earlier events in their lives through songs of their youth. And one of the people responsible for coming to see the therapeutic uses of music was Reverend Harford.

He ended his ecclesiastical career as a minor canon at Westminster Abbey. But what is significant for this tale is not where he ended his time in the church but where he began it. For it was here in Croydon in 1858 that he served his curacy, as we can read in the 1860 Crockford's Clerical Directory.

Frederick Kill Harford was born in 1832. His unusual middle name was his mother's family name. He was the second son of a well-to-do household from Clifton, just outside Bristol. They lived in number 22 Royal Crescent. He was educated at Rugby School and in 1850 entered New Inn Hall at Oxford to read Classics. He was awarded a BA in 1855 and his MA three years later. After his two year curacy here in Croydon, he was appointed as chaplain to the Bishop of Gibraltar. In 1861 he was appointed as a Minor Canon at Westminster Abbey where he remained in post until he died in 1906.

Frederick was always interested in the arts. In a diary written in 1859 by Maria Fox Trickett, a neighbour of the family in Clifton, she describes how ...'Mrs Harford sent Mama a Poem by her son, beautifully got up in Medieval style - & called The Martyrs of Lyons and Vienne, by the Reverend Frederick Harford MA.' Frederick continued to return to visit his West Country roots for many years. In the burial records of the district of Frenchay in the parish of Winterbourne, Gloucester, he is recorded as carrying out a funeral service in 1860, and again in 1868 when he officiated on two separate occasions. It would not be beyond reason to think that these were people known to the family who specifically asked Frederick to return and take the funeral service.

Having been recorded in this diary as having some talent for writing verse, it is fascinating how his ability developed. Even earlier, while he was at Rugby School, he won a prize for writing a poem about the River Niger. Later in his life, Frederick, now a clergyman with an interest in verse, turned his attention to hymn writing. Collecting these together, he published in 1894, 'Hymns for the Passing Hours, to suit family worship. Being arranged for one, two or three voices, with Responsoria."

Exactly when he started to believe that music had particular healing and soothing qualities is not certain. What is known is that in the early 1890s he founded and developed the Guild Of St Cecilia, a group of musicians dedicated to taking music into hospitals and other medical institutions so that patients could listen. Harford was described as an accomplished musician and Chapters of the Guild would gather in groups of 10 or so to play. The exact extent of the benefits of listening to music were not known or understood at this time, however, it was observed that the patients felt a real lift from this service. The Guild decided that the musicians should perform unseen by the patients, so they were placed behind a curtain. This was so there was an ethereal quality to the performance, with music coming from afar.

Whilst the Guild has long since ceased to function, the idea that music can help in all sorts of therapeutic ways has thrived. Frederick wasn't the only one to have had this idea, but he certainly played a significant part in the beginning of the movement. He was always convinced of the merits of music in medicine and wrote in a medical journal of the day that when he had performed in St Pancras' Infirmary. One female patient there said that she enjoyed the playing of a lullaby and staff remarked that this was the first time this woman had spoken in a fortnight. The St Cecilia Choir of which Frederick became so proud grew so large that they had to rehearse in the largest available room in the Westminster Palace Hotel. He invited any doctors or nurses who wished to come along and act as critics!

Frederick enjoyed a wide interest in the arts in general, not confining himself to music. He developed a friendship with Gustav Dore, the French painter, who he met at a dinner party in Sydenham where the artist was staying having visited the Great Exhibition of 1851 in Crystal Palace. One of Dore's most well known paintings, entitled 'Christ quittant le prettoir' (Christ leaving the praetorium), owes much of its development to Frederick's ideas. Dore was excited by the debates about the how Christ could be portrayed in the time between his trial and the taking up of his cross and subsequently spent ten years on this work. Gustav Dore, who died in 1883, regarded this particular painting as his masterpiece.

Frederick died on 11 November 1906 at 4a Dean's Yard, by Westminster Abbey, having never married. There was an entry in a London paper shortly after his passing, stating that if anybody felt they had any claim to his estate, they were to contact the appropriate solicitor. He might have died in relative obscurity but the music therapy profession owes him a real debt of gratitude.

A staccato Note about Derek Holman

Derek was the organist of Croydon Parish Church from 1958 to 1965. Before his appointment here he was assistant organist at St Paul's Cathedral up in London.

He made a particularly rich contribution to the musical life of Croydon, combining his musical duties for the church with his work with the Royal School of Church Music in Addington and it was he who in 1960, founded the Croydon Bach Choir.

After he left Croydon, he emigrated to Canada where he taught in the University of Toronto and became a well known and respected figure in Canadian music. He held many musical posts both in churches and for various musical groups. He was particularly noted for his work with the Canadian Childrens' Opera Chorus for whom he wrote an opera entitled Dr Canon's Cure. He composed many pieces of music including an arrangement of the well-known seasonal song, **Sir Christemas**

A sustained Note about Thomas Miller

Thomas Miller was a distinguished member of Croydon church and a significant figure in the local community during the late 18th century and into the early 19th century, and an organist.

You can find the name of Thomas Miller etched onto the dedication plaque under the window to the right of the north door in Croydon Minster. However, he would, I am sure, prefer to be remembered through music.

Thomas was the first person to play upon the Avery organ that was built and installed in 1794. That organ, which was sadly lost in the fire of 1867, was said to be the very best in Surrey and had a particularly sweet sound. After the fire, that organ's replacement was repositioned in the choir area at the church's eastern end, where it remains today. The Avery organ Thomas knew was at the opposite end of the church, high up above the west door of the building, together with a musicians' gallery.

But what of Thomas' life before and after the new organ was installed? He was born in 1768, the son of the Reverend Thomas Miller who was the rector of Wormshill, Kent, from 1767 until his death in 1792. Our Thomas went up to Trinity

College Cambridge when he was 18 and proved himself to be an especially intelligent scholar. He was awarded the Chancellor's medal along with his BA in 1791, was made a Fellow in 1793 and he gained his MA in 1794.

In the notes of the Cantab. Alumni it actually states that Thomas was said to be 'the best classical student in Europe.' The notes go on to add that 'he had many pupils whom he prepared for university, most of them being sons of well known men.' Perhaps more relevant to our tale, the notes then continue: 'Thomas was extremely musical. He could tune a piano without having had any teaching and could name offhand any notes sounded in any complicated chord on any instrument." Perfect pitch, then! His musical interests were developed further at Cambridge, as he was one of the founders of the Cambridge University Music Society.

Having moved to Croydon after his university days, Thomas spent the rest of his life here as a solicitor. He married Rebecca, who was the daughter of Samuel Dales. Thomas was active in promoting his Christian faith, and the

1826 report of the Society for the Promotion of Christian Knowledge (SPCK) includes the name of Thomas Miller of Croydon donating one guinea. This report also tells us that he lived in Church Street, although there is no house number written down. The house in Church Street is also mentioned in his will as 'he leves the property to his wife.'

By the time of his death. Thomas had amassed a considerable fortune through his solicitor's practice. His will stated that upon his death his wife was to receive the sum of one thousand pounds (a very large sum at the time) immediately. Thomas's name was also found on a list of subscribers to an extended sermon written by Rev Kemp and published in 1843 by Bell and Wood about the differences between scripture and Calvinism.

We know Thomas and Rebecca had one daughter, Anne, as well as two sons. George was born in 1815, and was called to the bar to commence his legal career in 1843. Another son, Edward, also went up to Trinity College Cambridge. He was ordained priest in Bristol in 1824 and served as vicar of Bognor from 1838-1877. Thomas' musical abilities were passed on to one of George's sons, Charles Edward Miller, who was to become organist of Lambeth Parish Church. Edward was to win composition prizes from the Madrigal Society, the best known of these being for the 8 part piece, 'Charm me asleep'. The same grandson also composed the hymn tune 'Waldrons', giving it a Croydon link as this is the name of an attractive street not too far from the Minster. He still has a Te Deum in D in current publishing lists.

Thomas his grandfather was vital to the development of church music here in Croydon. It was he who sponsored the young organist Thomas Walmisley to go to Cambridge. John Pyke Hullah, who was organist after Walmisley, lodged in one of Thomas's houses, describing Mr Miller as 'a man of culture'. And in William Streane's book on the history of Croydon, we read after Thomas' death in 1855 that 'the deceased was a gentleman of considerable musical abilities and was the first person to officiate at the organ erected in 1794, and destroyed in the fire. Mr Miller filled the post of organist for some years without fee or reward.'

It was also at this time that Croydon Parish Church engaged the renowned bass singer, James Bartleman, to be the church organist.

Thomas must have continued to fill in for Mr Bartleman on the occasions when he away singing in other parts of the country or when he was unwell, as the latter was unfortunately a man of poor health.

Thomas loved the church and he loved his music; that was his true epitaph and lasting legacy.

A staccato Note about Roy Massey

Roy was another of the Minster's organists who also worked at the Royal School of Church Music, where he was the Warden. He was organist here from 1965 to 1968.

Roy's promotion after he left was to be organist at Birmingham Cathedral and Musical Director for King Edward's School in that city. This was a particularly pleasing appointment for Roy as it took him back to the city of his birth and where he had been educated.

Awarded an MBE IN 1997, he became organist and Master of the Choristers at Hereford Cathedral from 1974 until 2001. Whilst at Hereford, Roy was responsible for a vast number of recordings and broadcasts. Roy is also very well known for his work as a conductor for the Three Choirs Festival.

A sustained Note about Thomas Walmisley

A gifted yet troubled man who was later to become a professor of music at Cambridge University, Thomas was appointed church organist in Croydon at the age of just 16.

As both Minster and Parish Church, the building in central Croydon has long had a reputation for great music making. Walk down to look at the board by the organ in the choir area and you can see that many well known musicians began their careers in this church.

Looking at the list of former organists, you can see Peter Nardone, now music director at Worcester Cathedral, Carl Jackson, now music director at the Chapel Royal Hampton Court Palace and Nigel McClintock, now music director at Belfast Cathedral. But the organist's tale which will be told here is about an organist of this church, from 1830 to 1833,

whose name does not appear on that board as only organists since the re-opening of the church after the fire are recorded.

In 1830, Thomas Attwood Walmisley, at just 16 years old, was appointed organist of this church. He was a son of Thomas Walmisley and his wife Mary Ann, the eldest of twelve children, and had been born on 21 January 1814. Thomas' father was an organist and his godfather, Thomas Attwood, was a composer. Between them, they tutored young Thomas in his music.

He was organist here for just three years before he went up to Cambridge. Studying at Trinity College, he was awarded a MA in music in 1841 and later a doctorate in 1848. During this time of study he must have been extremely busy as he simultaneously held the position of organist at both Trinity and St John's Colleges. He was a prodigious worker, his services as organist occupying him on Sundays at one time from 7.15am in the morning to 6.15pm in the evening.

In 1836 he was appointed Professor of Music at Cambridge University, a post he held until his death in 1856. One source described him as a champion of Bach, but prone to depression. Another source suggests his early death was the result of his excessive drinking.

He later moved to Hastings for the benefit of his health but it is here that he died. He is buried in the churchyard of St Andrew's Church, Fairlight, just along the Sussex coast.

A local source understood that Walmisley was introduced to the area by a fellow Cambridge professor and his wife who are also buried in the same churchyard.

His father edited much of his music, publishing the majority of his output after his death. He is remembered at Trinity College with a brass plaque in the chapel. 'The snare is broken and we are delivered,' it says on his memorial: the words are from Psalm 124 verse 7, written in chant form as befits a musician.

Walmisley is largely remembered today for his Evening Canticles, the Magnificat and Nunc Dimittis in D minor and a part song entitled Music All Powerful. He composed other Anglican liturgical settings, twenty two anthems, organ concertos, three string quartets and two sonatinas for oboe and piano. He also left behind a large number of vocal works, both sacred and secular. Trinity College noted that his music attracted admiration when he set an ode written by Wordsworth to music, on the occasion of Prince Albert's installation as Chancellor in 1847.

Despite his works still being sung in Anglican churches and cathedrals today, Walmisley never succeeded as a composer in his lifetime in the way he had hoped. The composer Mendelssohn was not very complimentary about his first symphony, when asked about it. Nevertheless, when you hear a piece of his music again, you must marvel at the prodigious talent he must surely have had to be appointed organist here at the Minster at the tender age of 16.

A staccato Note about Michael Fleming

Michael was the Minster's organist from 1968-78. He also worked at the RSCM as a tutor. After a series of prestigious organists' job after he leaving the Minster, he returned to Croydon in 1998 to become organist at St Michael's.

Whilst at Chingford in Essex, Michael had as his organ teacher Harold Darke of In the Bleak Midwinter fame. His career was always closely linked with hymnology, and he himself also wrote and arranged many hymn tunes of which I shall highlight two: **Palace Green**, a hymn tune for Sing praise to God who reigns above, and **Wellington**, written as an advent hymn for Lift up your heads ye mighty gates.

A Note about Martin How MBE, sustained to the present day

With a long and distinguished musical career to his name, Martin is the current Organist Laureate for Croydon Minster.

Back in the 1930s, in the days before the Second World War and then into the conflict itself, there lived two teachers. One was called Miss Keene, the other Miss Lax - by rather delightful coincidence. They came from opposite ends of the country, for the former worked in a Dame School in Brighton, the latter in Holm Park prep school in Moffat, Dumfriesshire. Neither knew each other and certainly they never met. Both, however, were dedicated professionals who looked to do the very best for the pupils in their charge. Both could be described as being 'ahead of their time.' They were nurturers and developers, not pen-pushers or bureaucrats.

Little did Miss Keane realise that a chord sequence she wrote for a 6 year old pupil in response to his request to be given some chords to play would still be remembered and played by that individual over 70 years later.

And Miss Lax, I am confident, had no idea that when she wrote for a third time to persuade some sceptical parents to let their son resume piano lessons, the positive response which eventually arrived was to be a pivotal moment for a scholar who was to go on and spend a career in music. These are the sorts of teachers that every parent would like their children to meet in school. These ladies were educationalists who, when they saw potential, would go that extra mile for their pupils.

Miss Keene did not have to produce an original mini musical composition of chords, as she in fact did in response to her pupil's request. She could just have found something in a music book. Miss Lax could have given up after receiving the first reply from the parents refusing to give consent for their son to resume piano lessons. That both teachers acted as they did helped to mould the early musical experiences of their pupil, Martin How. The award of an MBE in 1993 for his lifetime of service to Church Music through the Royal School of Church Music was a fitting reward for a gentleman who used his professional life in music to continue the very same nurturing and helping that he had experienced. Martin sought to give youngsters the chance to sing, something of which he had almost been deprived himself owing to the war preventing him from attending Choir School. Nowadays, more than ever, he is able to enjoy his music. He can be found most mornings in Croydon Minster, first having his own quiet time before sitting either at the organ or the piano playing or composing.

Two significant events in Martin's life brought about his meeting with each of these two remarkable teachers. The first was that because of his mother's ill-health and then death when he was just six years old, he and his sister Ruth were sent to a Boarding Dame school in Brighton. The second was his father's appointment as the Bishop of Glasgow resulting in the family's later relocating north of the border, where Martin was sent to Holm Park School.

It was during this period of re-location, before starting at the new school, that Martin gave up practising the piano and no longer showed any interest in continuing to play. Thus Martin's father and step-mother were sceptical when they received his letter asking to resume piano lessons. But, as we now know, it was the persistence of Miss Lax who persuaded both of them to have a change of heart.

Martin feels that this was the biggest turning point in his whole musical education. The prep school supplied the choir for the local Episcopal Church, the 'Tin Tabernacle' (to use Martin's description), and it was for its choir that Martin composed his first real tune. This was a single chant. It might have been simple, but it worked. This is a theme which is highlighted in Martin's successes with church choirs in his later career. Although Martin can still hear the clear tones of Miss Lax insisting that he do his practice on the piano, he was able to begin to improvise when he was at the keyboard. Although slightly bemused, Miss Lax recognised a talent.

His success at Holm Park paved the way for him to go to Repton School, Derbyshire, at the age of 13, being awarded a music scholarship in his second term. This was a school with a fine musical tradition. At Repton, Martin was able to achieve a notable musical ambition. Whilst living in Glasgow his main source of music was to listen to the gramophone with its old 78 records, of which his favourite was a recording of Mendelssohn's 'Hear my Prayer' sung by Ernest Lough, the famous boy soprano. In his first term at Repton, Martin saw that 'Hear my Prayer' was to be performed and that soloists were required. With his voice not yet broken, he auditioned and was chosen to sing the very piece he had performed endlessly in his own front room in Glasgow and had longed to sing in public. The chapel at Repton was to be the venue where his voice could be heard aloud!

One aspect of music that Martin especially appreciated at Repton was congregational singing on a big scale. The settings of the canticles for the Sunday services contained special parts for the congregation and Martin began to understand the impact of this sort of music making.

As he neared the end of his time at Repton, Martin was not sure of the pathway he should take in the future. His father, having the experience to research the rather complicated and not very well-advertised ways of appointing organ scholars, found the colleges which were currently seeking such a person. Martin was successful in his interview and duly started his three year position at Clare College, Cambridge.

When Martin arrived in Cambridge, the enormity of the job hit him on day one. There was no handover from the previous incumbent to show him the ropes. He was solely responsible for the music in the chapel. He found a notice board and duly pinned up the first request for a choir practice so he could have an idea of the resources at his disposal. A benevolent and tactful Old Reptonian immediately came to Martin's room and told him: 'I say, old chap, if you don't mind my saying so, we normally spell choir practice with a c!' 'I never was much of an academic,' Martin says.

Receiving much support from the loveable college Dean, Reverend Charlie Moule, an eminent New Testament scholar, Martin came to realise that he had other gifts to offer as well as his music. The modern word for his skill is 'outreach.' Martin had to make connections with local schools, have advertisements placed in local newspapers, all to build up his group of singers and musicians. In this he was successful and this trademark of involving and motivating a whole range of singers in his work was to be of particular importance throughout his professional career and into his retirement. He also spent much time running for the university's cross country team and nearly got a 'blue.'

After leaving Clare College, he did two years' National Service in the Royal Army Service Corps, where he was awarded a commission and eventually became a lieutenant. Martin often says that his army training was useful in so many ways. He then worked for the Royal School of Church Music at Addington Palace, Croydon, as choirmaster to its college, supervising students and the three boys' choirs.

After three years there, Martin returned to Cambridge in 1960 to complete his degree, with a year studying theology.

This was Martin's one year of intense study with not much music. He found it deeply rewarding in terms of his personal understanding and faith. Martin returned to the Royal School of Church Music in 1964, following a three year stint as choirmaster at Grimsby Parish Church, where he built up the number of boys from 14 to 32 and started its 'travelling choir' which visited churches across the county on Saturdays for demonstrations and special services. He then remained with the RSCM in one capacity or another until his retirement in 1993.

It was during these latter years with them that Martin composed music for the huge number of events he was attending across the south of England as its commissioner. When he was 12, you may recall that he had composed a single chant for his prep school choir. He knew his own ability and he knew his resources. The same process was needed in these new circumstances. Martin describes it as 'composing little tunes' for 'little choirs' with 'limited resources.' That he was so successful in doing this was down to three things.

Firstly, not having perfect pitch, he knew that if he couldn't sing his own melodies and harmony lines well, then others couldn't either. Secondly, his style of working to inform and motivate young singers via the Chorister Training Scheme was appreciated and recognised by all. Thirdly, he realised that by bringing in these 'little choirs' to sing with larger resources, the singers would be inspired and raise their own standards accordingly.

This was done mostly through one day choir events, choir visits and courses.

Now, having been retired for well over 20 years, Martin can look back on what he has achieved. As he says: 'I never decided that I would go in for a career in music. I just discovered that I had.' Martin How has been part of the music scene at Croydon Minster since 1993 when he retired from the RSCM. He was tentatively invited by the Minster's then musical director, Peter Nardone, to become assistant organist. Martin accepted and was glad to be able to do more organ playing again and to have a regular church of his own to attend. 23 years later, he's pleased to say: 'Now I am retired, I have the time to really enjoy music.' This is a profound statement from a man who, throughout his professional life, fostered in those around him a deep enjoyment of music, especially choral music.

Listed among his favourite composers are Vaughan Williams, Herbert Howells, E.J. Meoran, Gerald Finzi and Claude Debussy. Since his retirement, Martin has written four seasonal cantatas, several piano suites with which he is particularly pleased and a series of organ pieces called Gospel Colours. 'I am not that great', he says, 'with rhythms or counterpoint but rather better, perhaps, at melody and harmony where my clichés are well known.' This is the way Martin describes much of his own output.

In 2016 he performed at the piano, to great acclaim, musical portraits of his friends as part of the fourth Croydon Heritage Festival. He has a book of his own organ compositions, Organ Album, to which he constantly returns.

In January 2017 he composed a work for piano, organ and voice to mark 150 years since Croydon Minster was also completely destroyed in a fire caused by a malfunctioning gas heater. The original building on the site was Saxon and filled with monuments and memorials, some of which were later restored after sustaining severe damage, but many of which were lost forever. Among the saddest losses was of course John Avery's famous organ. The commemorative concert took place on Saturday 7th January 2017.

There is a story that the excellent vintage Broadwood piano that now he plays in the church was once owned by Charles Lloyd, the organist of Christ Church Oxford before Basil Harwood, the two directors of the choir when his father sung as a chorister. If proved true, the picture of Martin How playing the piano around which his father may well have stood singing in Oxford is such a poignant one.

But then, much of what Martin has achieved in music has a poignancy about it. Here is a humble and sincere man who has encouraged others to love music and to participate in it. His words, as well as his music, have been both comforting and challenging to a great many people. His own faith has been a constant source of strength throughout his life.

'I have been very lucky,' says Martin. 'God moves in mysterious ways......'

Miss Keene and Miss Lax, you would be so proud of how your young pupil turned out.

www.ingramcontent.com/pod-product-compliance
Lightning Source LLC
Chambersburg PA
CBHW071010080526
44587CB00015B/2410